[Crow

NOTES FROM THE FRONT.

COLLATED BY THE GENERAL STAFF.

LONDON:

Published and © by the
The Naval & Military Press
in association with the Royal Armouries

Unit 10 Ridgewood Industrial Park,
Uckfield, East Sussex, TN22 5QE
Tel: +44 (0) 1825 749494
Fax: +44 (0) 1825 765701

MILITARY HISTORY AT YOUR FINGERTIPS
www.naval-military-press.com
ONLINE GENEALOGY RESEARCH
www.military-genealogy.com
ONLINE MILITARY CARTOGRAPHY
www.militarymaproom.com

In reprinting in facsimile from the original, any imperfections are inevitably reproduced and the quality may fall short of modern type and cartographic standards.

TACTICAL NOTES.

Notes from a General Officer at the Front.

(a.) GENERAL.

1. *Defensive positions.*—One of the principal lessons of the war, hitherto, from a tactical point of view, is the necessity for screening positions for defence from the enemy's artillery fire. The enemy's artillery is numerous, powerful and efficient, and our infantry has suffered much from its fire. The German infantry, on the other hand, is inferior to our own in developing fire effect. A short field of fire (500 yards or even less) has been found sufficient to check a German infantry attack. Tactically, therefore, in occupying ground for defence, every effort should be made to combine the fire of our own guns and rifles against the enemy's infantry, while denying to the enemy the use of his artillery by the siting of trenches in positions which it is intended to hold on to, behind rather than on the crest line or forward slopes.

This does not mean that advanced posts have been found to be of no value. On the contrary, in order that full advantage may be taken of the strength of such positions as described above, it has been found essential to prevent the enemy's rapid approach by the use of advance posts supported by artillery, in order to gain time for deployment and the reconnaissance of the main position, and under favourable conditions for its entrenchment.

2. *Protective troops.*—It was found necessary during the retreat to provide for the protection of a large body of troops such as a corps by means of protective detachments, flank and rear guards, rather than by an outpost line only. We had not been accustomed to handle large bodies of troops in peace time, and in the early days relied entirely on outposts for protection. It was found that the long range and power of the enemy's artillery kept the troops in constant anxiety of being shelled in their bivouacs, and that when pressed by the enemy in retreat the main bodies were easily brought to action and delayed. When protective detach-

ments at a distance from the main bodies were employed, the troops rested in greater security and were able to resume the march confident in the ability of the rear guard to hold the enemy off unless very heavily pressed. These protective detachments at a distance from the main body have been found to be especially necessary in the absence of protective cavalry. When this system is combined with billeting in depth a march can be resumed at any moment without delay, and mobility is greatly increased.

3. *Passage of rivers.*—Several rivers have been crossed both in advance and in retreat, and experience has been gained both in forcing the passage of a river and in delaying the enemy on a river line. In forcing the passage of a river defended by the enemy's rear guard it may be useful to remind subordinate commanders that there should be no delay in engaging the enemy at the point or points that he is defending and reconnoitring at once for a point of passage which is undefended. Sometimes boats, rafts, a bridge the enemy has forgotten, a weir or other means of crossing have been found. When a sufficient force has been passed over by such means, the enemy, who frequently offers a strong opposition at the defended points, using quite a small force with several machine guns, can be quickly cleared out and a bridge thrown. The Royal Engineers should reconnoitre at once for the most favourable site for a bridge, and can often find and collect materials to supplement the available pontoons. Those with the field companies have twice been found insufficient for the purpose, and the bridging train may not be at hand.

In the event of its being desired to delay the passage of a river by the enemy, it may not be out of place to draw attention to the necessity for studying the bends of the river and the topographical features of the banks, with a view to ascertaining the likely points at which the enemy will try to cross, and making tactical dispositions accordingly. The re-entrant bends towards the enemy should be brought under artillery fire by establishing observation posts from which they can be seen and artillery fire directed upon them. The throwing of a bridge may thus be prevented or it may be destroyed after it has been thrown. Detachments should be posted in advance of any main position that it may be intended to occupy, to prevent the enemy from debouching from the necks of these bends, if he succeeds in crossing. If dispositions of this nature are made with skill the enemy may be delayed for a considerable time, and if desired, time can be gained to prepare a position for defence.

4. *Night operations.*—This corps has not carried out any night attacks, but it has been attacked at night, and it has been found that the enemy apparently makes all his arrangements beforehand and usually advances in strength, dispensing with scouts or advanced parties. No warning is therefore given of his attack and to meet it picquets must be strong and on the position on which they intend to resist. There is no time to rouse them and occupy trenches. If a picquet is watching a road at night, the road should be barricaded and the picquet placed so as to bring fire to bear on the road in front of the barricade, and should never be placed in a position where it can be rushed unprotected by an obstacle.

5. *Formations when on the move.*—It has been found that the long range of the enemy's artillery combined at times with the weakness or even the absence of our own cavalry has rendered the infantry of advanced guards particularly liable to come under artillery fire in close formation. Not only do the troops themselves suffer on these occasions, but the first line transport has been found to be especially vulnerable. It is very undesirable that the march of the main bodies should be delayed by the constant deployment of advanced guards to avoid casualties. It is, therefore, essential, when the front is inadequately covered by cavalry, that troops should be able rapidly to adopt formations suitable when under artillery fire, and they should be trained to adopt these formations as quickly as possible. No more first line transport vehicles than are absolutely necessary should march with an advanced guard, and it has been found desirable to divide first line transport into two echelons.

When troops are fighting, first line transport, first line wagons of artillery, field ambulances and ammunition columns should beware of the deceptive shelter afforded by villages. The enemy's high-explosive shell render villages and the vicinity of buildings especially dangerous. Wounded should not be placed in a church during an action. Vehicles and horses should not be crowded together near points that are easily ranged upon by the map, such as barns, haystacks, and road crossings.

6. *March discipline.*—Men who have not been with the colours during the last 4 or 5 years do not understand the necessity for good march discipline. It should be impressed upon all ranks and should be resolutely insisted upon at all training previous to arrival in the theatre of war. There has been straggling, no doubt in great measure due to exhaustion during the first phase, but it is most necessary to tighten up the march discipline again and to prevent undue opening out and straggling.

Horsed wagons should not be parked on the road.

Wagons should never be halted when passing through a village.

When a halt is necessary it should be made before reaching or after passing a village.

Men accompanying trains should carry their rifles and should march in formed bodies.

Each unit should detail an officer with a small party of selected non-commissioned officers and men to march in rear of the unit in order to enforce orders against straggling, leaving the ranks for water, and so forth.

7. *Concealment from aircraft.*—The enemy's aircraft are numerous and efficient, and it is clear that he obtains by this or other means excellent information as to our movements. It has been found impossible to conceal movements of large bodies of troops when on the march from this observation, and the position of large bivouacs can always be observed from the air. But much can be done to conceal artillery positions and trenches, and the use of overhead cover, as we know from our own experience, makes it difficult to ascertain from the air whether trenches and gun emplacements are occupied or not. Troops should therefore be taught to understand the necessity for concealment from aircraft whenever the conditions admit of it.

8. *Machine guns.*—Machine guns have played a very important part in the war, and the enemy is adept in making use of their surprise effect, which has been found to be very great indeed. Till they are located and engaged machine guns play havoc with troops in close order, but when located they are easily knocked out by artillery fire,

or silenced by a concentrated rifle fire. Great care should therefore be taken in selecting the positions for machine guns, in occupying them without attracting attention and in reserving fire till a suitable opportunity arrives, in order to make full use of their surprise effect. The only way to avoid the surprise effect of the enemy's machine guns is by careful reconnaissance.

(b.) DIVISIONAL MOUNTED TROOPS.

9. *Reconnaissance duties.*—The mounted troops allotted to army corps are strictly limited in numbers and consist of a squadron of cavalry and a cyclist company with each division. Experience has shown that army corps cannot always rely on receiving protection from cavalry, nor can they be sure that information which is essential will be obtained for them by cavalry or even aircraft. In these circumstances there are many duties to be performed by the divisional mounted troops, and if the strictest economy is not employed they will soon become depleted in numbers both from casualties and exhaustion.

No reconnoitring detachment should be stronger than is necessary for its immediate purpose, and no reconnaissance should be sent further afield than is necessary to obtain the actual information required. The greatest care should be taken to limit the scope of these missions and to make instructions clear and definite.

Mounted men should not be kept out at night if it can be avoided.

(c.) ARTILLERY.

10. *Tactical handling of.*—Our artillery has suffered from certain disadvantages during the war so far. In the early battles it was outnumbered, while the ground on the Aisne has prevented its close co-operation with our infantry, which has consequently been exposed to a heavy artillery fire that our guns have been unable to cope with, except with the assistance of aerial observation. The enemy's heavy howitzers have been more numerous than and superior, as regards weight of metal, to our own heavy artillery. The result has been that our infantry have suffered heavy losses from the enemy's artillery fire, and the efforts of our own artillery have necessarily been directed primarily towards neutralizing its effect.

The conclusion has been drawn by some that this should be its primary rôle. There could be no greater mistake. It should be our constant endeavour to rectify this position and, while developing the power of our artillery, to improve our tactical skill in handling it, so that it is not constantly on the defensive, and so that we may employ its power primarily in attacking the enemy's infantry, and so reverse the situation. As already indicated above the first essential to this end in defence is the skilful use of ground. It is hoped that the Army will soon pass to the offensive and that the artillery will then have an opportunity of showing its ability to support its infantry closely and devotedly in attack. Undoubtedly one of the chief lessons of the war has been the necessity for the closest co-operation between the two arms.

11. *Concealment of.*—Concealment has been forced upon our artillery. The enemy's fire is rapid and accurate, and the effects of the high explosive shell from his heavy howitzers is very damaging, not only to personnel but to material as well. Flashes must be concealed from the front and observation posts selected with the greatest care, and occupied with caution. Emplacements must, whenever possible, be concealed from aerial observation by overhead cover, branches or straw.

12. *Cover for.*—Protection must be provided for the detachments, and, if the situation permits, it is advisable to prepare the emplacements before occupying the position.

13. *Observation by.*—For accurate shooting, effective observation is essential. Forward observation must be used, and for this purpose telephones are invaluable, and great care should be taken of them. Telephone wire should be husbanded.

Visual signalling has been little used.

14. *Co-operation with aircraft.*—Great strides have been made in the co-operation between aircraft and artillery for the purpose of locating hostile trenches and guns and observation of fire. No battery can now be considered really efficient that is not able to range rapidly and accurately by means of aerial observation. The system of coloured lights works well. The new wireless apparatus is better.

A 4

15. *Anti-aircraft guns.*—The anti-aircraft gun plays an important part, and if skilfully handled both tactically and as regards shooting should be able to prevent the close reconnaissance of a specified area, or the co-operation of the enemy's aircraft with his artillery. Efforts should therefore be made to develop the skill of the personnel.

16. *Ammunition.*—The expenditure of 60-pr. and 4·5 howitzer ammunition while on the river Aisne has been very heavy. New formations arriving in the theatre of war should be especially cautioned not to waste ammunition of these natures. In battles of position these weapons are evidently destined to play an important part.

17. *Ammunition columns.*— Roads have often been blocked during operations by ammunition columns. Officers in command of these units should be cautioned to park their horse drawn vehicles off the roads whenever possible.

(d.) INFANTRY.

18. *Siting of trenches.*—Owing to the accuracy of the enemy's artillery fire, it is desirable that ground which is to be held defensively or to assist further advance should be entrenched. Trenches should be commenced at once with the light entrenching tool and improved later as opportunity occurs. They should be deep and narrow and should show above the ground level as little as possible, and all trenches should be traversed at intervals of five to ten rifles. When siting trenches it should be borne in mind that the enemy is adept at bringing enfilade artillery fire to bear from flank positions. At any point, such as a salient, at which trenches are particularly liable to this form of fire, great care should be taken as to their siting and they should be especially heavily traversed. Where head cover cannot be provided, cover from shell fire for the troops when not actually using their rifles, can readily be obtained by making recesses in the trenches on the side nearest to the enemy. It has been found that head-cover or anything that in any way interferes with the rapid use of the rifle is a disadvantage in positions where the trenches have a short field of fire and are therefore liable to be rushed. If immunity from shrapnel fire can be obtained up to the moment of having to resist the infantry attack, no more can be hoped for. Communication trenches for supports and ammunition supply are necessary

and they should be wide enough to permit of a stretcher being carried along them so as to facilitate the removal of wounded.

Support trenches may be close to the firing line trenches, but should be so made that the men can lie down and sleep. All trenches must be assimilated to the surroundings.

Elbow rests have not generally been found useful.

Protection against high-explosive shells of howitzers is unobtainable in field operations, but this effect can be localized by traverses.

19. *Observation by aeroplane.*—As soon as it appears that troops have been located by an aeroplane their position should be changed, as it has been found by experience that batteries open fire directly the aeroplane report has been received.

20. *Enemy's ruses.*—The enemy adopts all manner of ruses to deceive our troops such as the use of the white flag, or dressing up in the uniforms of the Allies. It is important therefore that any body of troops approaching our lines should be brought to a halt at some distance from them and one individual only be allowed to advance to establish their *bona fides.* Should they refuse to halt, or act in a suspicious manner, they should, irrespective of their dress or of the circumstances under which they approach, be fired upon without hesitation.

21. *Standing to arms.*—Troops in contact with the enemy should always stand to arms before dawn ready to move off and should remain under arms till the front is reported by patrols to be clear.

22. *Fixing bayonets.*—The enemy's attacks develop so quickly that it is important that troops, and especially protective detachments, should fix bayonets before the final stages are reached. At night, outposts and troops in trenches should have their bayonets permanently fixed. When attacking at night bayonets should always be fixed at the position of deployment.

Extracts from letters received from General Officers at the Front.

Cavalry.—Up to the present long distance reconnaissance by cavalry has been entirely replaced by aeroplanes, the cavalry work being confined to covering the immediate

(11111)   B front, or to being massed for operations against a flank. The training of the cavalry with the rifle has been invaluable, and has given them great advantage over the enemy. There have been no cases up to the present of large cavalry charges with the *arme blanche*, but the latter has been used a good deal in small affairs.

Infantry.—The choice of infantry fields of fire is largely governed by the necessity for avoiding exposure to artillery fire. A field of fire of 300 to 500 yards is quite sufficient. This indicates the necessity for accurate shooting at short ranges. Insist on the training of scouts, and particularly on the training of non-commissioned officers as patrol leaders.

An advance should not be made in rigid lines, but with clouds of skirmishers—5 or 6 yards apart—thrown forward according to the ground and available cover.

The essential thing is to pay attention to the sound principles on which our training has been based.

Notes received from Officers at the Front regarding the work of Engineers.

1. Field Companies have been chiefly employed in—
   Bridge demolition.
   Bridge repair.
   Pontoon and trestle bridges.
   Pile driving.
   Making approaches.
   Assisting infantry in improving field defences.
   Wire obstacles.
   Preparing positions in rear of fighting line, utilizing civilian working parties.

2. The handling of explosives and pontooning (including heavy bridge) and Weldon trestle work should receive special attention.

3. As regards permanent bridge repairs to take mechanical transport it has sometimes been possible to patch up the disabled bridge. 25 sappers were able, in 60 men-hours, to make four girders 75 feet long, built of wood and iron tie rods obtained locally; these were successfully launched on to a broken pier and the bridge was restored for mechanical transport.

In another case a company drove in pile piers and put up 30 wooden girders to take mechanical transport.

A Field Squadron spliced a demolished steel girder bridge which had been cut through, but the ends of which had not fallen in ; the splicing was done with steel bars and chains, and the bridge took mechanical transport.

4. For notes regarding trench work, *see* under " Infantry."

5. *Signal Companies.*—Considerable use has been made of the permanent lines of the country. Motor cyclists have rendered valuable service, and have proved the chief means of communication during movement. It is essential that they should be expert at effecting ordinary "running repairs."

The telephone detachments have been invaluable ; messages are generally sent on the vibrator. During heavy shell fire it has been very difficult to hear the signals, but messages are sent and received between the bursts.

Helio', flag and lamp have all been used effectively on occasions ; but great care is necessary to conceal the signaller from the enemy, as when seen a heavy shell fire is directed on him. On one occasion the reinforcements of an infantry brigade were directed to the most hardly pressed point by flag signal from the back of a farm.

Notes from a conversation with a Battalion Commander who has recently been wounded and invalided home.

Entrenchments.—It has been found that the best form of entrenchment is a deep narrow trench without parapet or headcover. Parapet and headcover form too much of a mark for the German artillery. Trenches 2 feet wide for " fire standing," with the earth thrown in rear, are recommended. The difficulty of draining trenches has not been overcome. If possible, trenches should be dug to communicate with hollow lanes. When the men are once ensconced in these trenches they have little to fear. A company of the battalion under the informant was fired on all day by all types of German guns, and only one man was wounded. Battalions which have not dug themselves in at once have suffered in consequence.

Shallow trenches constructed with the portable tools are worse than no trenches at all against artillery fire, as they give the German artillery a better target.

When siting trenches by day it is better to occupy a position with a false crest on the enemy's side than to occupy a crest with no dead ground to the front. *See* Plate V., page 13.

Trenches sited at A will probably not suffer at all from hostile gun fire. Those at B will be " pounded " with great accuracy by hostile artillery.

From A only 1,000 yards field of fire is possible. Field of fire from B is anything up to 2 miles. Of the two A is by far the better, and the German artillery will find great difficulty in locating the trenches.

Electric torches have been found most useful by battalion and company-commanders who possess them. In siting trenches *at night* it is most useful to send out a man with an electric torch in front of the proposed trench. The man should hold the torch some 2 or 3 feet from the ground and should gradually move backwards towards the enemy. If this is not done, trenches may be made at night with perhaps a field of fire of only 50 yards.

Tools.—Infantry battalions have often been handicapped because the battalion picks and shovels were a long way in rear in a wagon, which has been unable to reach the battalion.

When a battalion is sent forward to secure an important point (*e.g.*, at the passage of a river) there should be at least 200 picks and shovels actually distributed amongst the men before they go forward. The small portable tools are useful, however, for improving a bank or ditch at the side of a road.

Every effort should be made to collect tools from the various farms in the vicinity.

It is essential that telephonic communication should be maintained between the forward infantry and the troops, especially the artillery, in rear.

It struck the informant that intercommunication between the front line and our own artillery is a matter which should receive continuous attention.

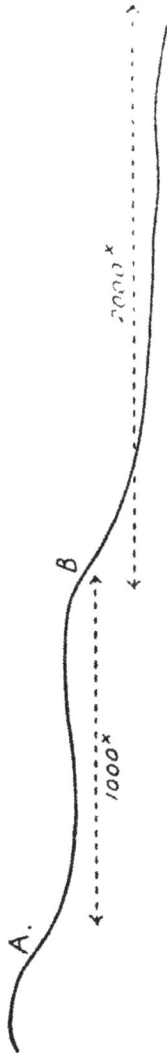

Plate V.

14

Operations in woods.—Our infantry would be much assisted if accompanied by a few mounted troops to do the scouting work when traversing woods. The woods have little undergrowth and numerous cross roads and paths.

Especially in rear-guard work the absence of mounted troops is likely to lead to infantry being intercepted by German machine guns and small bodies of mounted Uhlans, who hang on to a retiring force with great determination. These Uhlans are bold to excess and do a good deal of dismounted work.

Operations in woods call for the most deliberate preparation—a fact which is not always fully appreciated.

Outposts.—The importance of standing to arms an hour before daybreak is by no means fully appreciated. Naturally the exhaustion of the men is the difficulty in this. In the forward lines quarter to half the force is on outpost, and even in the third line back one-eighth of the troops are on outpost duty.

Billets.—The difficulty of finding officers at night in billets where they are covered up in straw, or on roads must be recognized. An adjutant must know exactly where the captain of each company is lying, so that he can wake him up without disturbing others. In the same way a battalion commander must sleep at a spot where the brigade-major can instantly find him.

Advance under artillery fire.—Several times it has been necessary to advance under unsubdued hostile artillery fire. Small columns at 50 yards interval and 300 yards distance have been found to be the best method of avoiding casualties. The 19th Brigade lying in the open in this formation were shelled by two batteries for half an hour and had only 25 casualties.

Extracts from a private letter from an Officer Commanding a Howitzer Battery.

*　　　*　　　*　　　*

1. Concealed positions are to be employed on nearly every occasion, batteries have been obliged on occasions to come

into the open, but the result has generally been a heavy casualty list.

2. The German fuzes are excellent, but the Germans waste much ammunition and have a tendency to burst too high. They go in for the moral effect of a continuous volume of fire, which certainly has the result they aim at for a short time, after which we have got to rather despise it.

3. I have had no opportunity of seeing much of the French artillery personally, but a battery was in action close to me one day. It was very quick and appeared to be very effective.

4. To say that artillery cannot stop an infantry advance by itself is sheer nonsense. The German infantry will not face our artillery fire, nor that of the French.

5. The Germans, I think, register a lot. They appear to me to do very little ranging, but generally bring effective fire to bear immediately our troops appear at certain points which apparently have been registered, they either "register" or else have an extraordinary range-taker.

6. The equipment is sticking it well, the No. 3 director and one-man range-finder much better than I anticipated. Even the despised telephone equipment has proved far from unsatisfactory. I have been in action now for 20 days— my observation station about 1,000 yards from the battery —and I have been in constant communication night and day with only two small breaks of 10 minutes each, due to the wire being cut by German shrapnel, a really remarkable performance. It all depends on the knowledge the operators have of the instruments, and I am lucky in the extreme.

7. The German infantry cannot touch ours and their shooting is deplorable. They seem to depend entirely on their machine guns, which are the very devil and magnificently handled.

8. The Germans are adepts at "ruses"—false observing stations, bogus trenches, &c.—we cannot hold a candle to them in this respect.

9. The Germans do much shooting by aeroplane observations with a certain amount of success. Their airmen are very bold.

10. The German artillery would appear to consist of—

15-pr. field gun, 3·03-inch.

A light field howitzer, approximately 4·2-inch.

A heavy field howitzer, approximately 5·9-inch.

An 8-in. mortar ? commonly known as "Black Maria",

a siege gun destined for the siege of Paris, but turned on to us here ; its effect is very local. It is wonderfully accurate, and the Germans can put shell after shell from it in very nearly the same position. It has a very long range, 12,000 yards and more.

11. We did not do enough shooting by the map at practice camps, *e.g.*, I frequently get an order "aeroplane has reported a 6-gun battery in action 400 yards south of the O in COURTECON, engage it", but we do not do much of this kind of shooting in camps. Map reading strikes me as being enormously important.

12. Given a good map, a battery, the flashes of which are visible, can be knocked out by a concealed battery ; I am proud to say I have done this on two occasions.

13. "Battery fire 1 second" with lyddite has a most disconcerting effect on a hostile battery, and will nearly always silence it if the approximate range has been found. Some batteries go in for a lot of salvoes, as also do the Germans.

14. The concealment of guns and wagon lines from air-craft observations is all-important ; units which have ignored this have suffered tremendously.

15. I had a very good series yesterday with aeroplane observation and wireless communication, and am reported to have got a hit with lyddite on a German battery at the 11th round—on this point I am sceptical.

16. In my opinion, in a retirement the 1st line wagons should remain with, or close to, the battery ; otherwise there is a tendency for them to get lost.

17. Obtaining the line of fire by magnetic bearing has been wonderfully successful ; I have used this means of obtaining the line more than any other.

Such are my experiences for what they are worth. I am convinced that concealment of guns is everything, and many of our casualties are due to the non-observance of this.

One more point has occurred to me, and that is the importance of lowering the angle of sight when searching behind a hill. Otherwise shell when they come over the crest line are miles in the air and comparatively inocuous.

Notes on Artillery in the present War, furnished by an Artillery Officer attached to General Headquarters.

Positions occupied.—With a few exceptions positions are completely covered, not only from view at the target end, but from possible air observation. The enemy possess large scale maps believed to be as large as 6-inch, and, as soon as guns are located by them, a severe fire is brought to bear immediately. It is on this account important to avoid always conspicuous or easily-identified points on the map. Ranging, as we understand it, is as often as not dispensed with altogether. Open and semi-covered positions possess no advantage over covered positions. They would only be occupied on emergency and with the knowledge that the battery would probably be destroyed sooner or later.

Positions of readiness are only to be considered if well concealed, but guns not required in action are better placed safe out of range.

Observing stations.—In the open position the choice appears to make little difference. If, however, occupied in the dark and the battery completely dug in, the battery commander is better on a flank clear of blast and smoke of enemy's high explosive shell. In covered positions the battery commander almost invariably observes from in front no matter what nature of gun. The distance, from 500 yards up to 1,000 and more, according to nature of operation and ground. Communication always by telephone. This, indeed, is the only possible means and endeavour is made to dig in the wire, perhaps with a plough.

In the event of wire being broken, recourse must be had to chain of orderlies. Megaphones are useful.

Obtaining the Line.—Two aiming posts seem to have been sometimes, but seldom, used. A battery angle is sent if

C

battery commander can see the battery ; but far more often
line is given roughly in a quick series or by compass or map
in a deliberate series. Trial shots are fired and correction
made as required. With heavy guns the method employed
is either the compass or direction given by a reference to a
map placed on a plane table, the latter the most popular.
Where possible, as in the operations on the Aisne, the 18-pr.
gun may be used to range for the 60-pr. to save ammunition.
There are many casualties to directors. The hand angle of
sight is a good deal used. Plotter never used and may be
dispensed with.

Battery headquarters is too large. Signallers and lookout
men are not wanted as a rule. Patrols and ground-scouts
never—*i.e.*, as part of the battery headquarters. The battery
commander has battery serjeant-major and a telephonist
with him, and perhaps a director man who will take a few
notes as penciller. The range-finder would be separately
dug in, if used at all, and two or three men possibly dug in
at intervals to pass orders on emergency. The ranging
officer with the battery is dug in, probably under a limber
in rear of line of guns, with telephone man. Section commanders are dug in close behind wagon bodies. The
consensus of opinion of battery commanders seems to be
decidedly against observation vehicles. They could only be
used on certain occasions and are difficult to drag into
position without being seen. Moreover, a battery commander
does not feel secure perched up on such a vehicle. He
prefers a tree or stack or building of some kind, or else to be
dug right in. Climbing irons or dogs, rope ladders, &c.,
would be of great use. German observatories are never seen
now ; they are effectually concealed if used.

Ranging.—The keynote is simplicity. Section ranging
with percussion—according to information at present available—is the method always used. It is not known if
collective has ever been used or not.

Objectives.—More information is necessary before a full
report can be made under this heading. Most batteries
have never seen any such target as troops in the open or
guns in any sort of position. There are exceptions, however,
and guns have had to deal with infantry columns crossing
the front, infantry advancing in large bodies—crowds—and
the rush of an infantry counter attack. In such cases the

18-pr. shrapnel is admitted on all sides as being most efficient. Time is certainly not the important factor that it is at practice. At the open pitched battles as at Mons and Cambrai, situations appear to have been considerably confused, and battery commanders were practically independent except those close to their own brigade headquarters. Telephone communication broke down at once owing to the wires being cut, and any orders that reached battery commanders came by mounted messenger. There appears to have been no visual signalling.

Gun targets.—At the battles just referred to there were cases of guns being located and even knocked out by shrapnel, but these seem to have been rare cases. The covered position is the one adopted and retained to the last. It must be clearly understood that the artillery duel is very much "en evidence." All arms and all ranks agree that the artillery dominates the situation on either side. Its effect is devastating where a target is visible, and infantry, where the strengths approximate to an equality, are quite unable to face it. All efforts are consequently made to establish a superiority in artillery. On the battlefield there is no sign of battle bar the few bursting shell and a few strips of newly-turned earth, which mark the infantry trenches. Not a man or a gun is visible unless some effort be made to test the strength of some corner of the field ; even then it will be invisible to nine-tenths of the front. The chief effort on either side is to locate the big guns by any means. We employ aeroplanes, but the enemy apparently employ an amazingly efficient secret service in addition. The aircraft are always at a height of about 6,000 feet if up at all, and there they appear to be immune from fire. The big gun positions are frequently changed—not less than every two or three days—but ours, however well concealed, are located to a yard by the hostile gunners, and 6-inch or 8-inch high explosive shell dropped right on the guns or in the pits. It is important that these big guns have alternative emplacements always ready for occupation at short notice, after dark, and these should always be irregularly placed with big intervals up to 100 yards, and at varying ranges of 50 yards or so. Inside a wood is often a suitable position. A megaphone in a wood carries well and assists section commanders in these difficult circumstances. Searchlights are hardly used at all. German balloons are always aloft, but our authorities are not in favour of these aids to observation, for reasons which have been thoroughly discussed.

The shooting of the German artillery can only be described as "uncanny." Occasionally great waste of ammunition takes place from, no doubt, faulty information, but parties of troops, whether gun teams, ammunition columns, bivouacs, billets and even headquarters of brigades and divisions have to make constant changes of their position or incur the penalty of having a dozen of the large shells dropped right into them without warning and when least expected. Dummy batteries, observation posts, &c., to deceive hostile aeroplanes, have proved valuable.

Seventy per cent. of our casualties are said to be due to artillery fire, and most of them to the high-explosive shell. The "error of the gun" appears to be nearly non-existent, and it is quite common to see four high-explosive heavy shells dropped within 2 or 3 yards of each other. It is difficult to find any explanation for this, possibly the design of shell has much to do with it. The enemy's time fuzes are also astonishingly accurate, particularly those of the field howitzers. Their shrapnel is far inferior to that of the 18-pr. This is admitted by all. There appear to be very few cases of shields having been hit by bullets. Casualties generally result from the backward effect of the high-explosive shell. These will quickly destroy a battery when located, but shrapnel from frontal fire never will.

Laying.—There is no direct laying. Our methods have well answered the test of war.

Methods of fire.—Gun fire is evidently very rare, battery fire is the usual method. The largest number of rounds fired by a battery in a day, according to present information, amounts to 1,152 for an 18-pr. battery, but the total number in the war is not double this for the same battery.

Control of fire.—Voice control has been employed in some of the somewhat confused actions referred to above. A howitzer battery on one occasion was engaged with infantry at 600 yards, firing shrapnel full charge; voice control was employed. Another battery, the day after disembarkation from the train, had to cover a front of over 180 degrees. It was shot at later from in rear also. Voice control was naturally used, but in the normal action it would never be considered for a minute.

Ammunition supply.—No very definite system has been evolved as being the best. As much cover as possible must be gained both from overhead and from behind if possible. Sometimes both wagons may conveniently be up, or wagon one side and limber the other side of the gun. Replenishment of ammunition is normally by carriers, but may be effected by wagons at night, &c. Limber supply does not appear to have been ordered, but the limber ammunition has often been used up.

Corrector.—Officers do not sufficiently use the table on page 164, Field Artillery Training. The cardinal fault of our shooting would appear to be bursting shrapnel too short ; the same applies to that of the enemy.

4·5-inch Q.F. Howitzers.—Never used in brigade at all, often by sections. Time shrapnel ranging with the howitzer is believed not to have been used at all.

60-pr. B.L. has been invaluable. Economy of ammunition is of first importance. It can sometimes be attained by making use of the 18-pr. for ranging purposes.

Entrenching.—Types in "Field Artillery Training" of pits, &c., are not sufficient. Pits for men must be at least 4 feet deep and narrow, but many battery commanders prefer the gun to be in a deep pit. It depends partly on the weather. It is desirable to have a parapet in rear as well as in front on account of the high explosive shell. Solid overhead cover is also desirable as far as possible. The width, 13 feet, is not excessive in bad ground or wet weather.

Map reading.—Map reading forms a very important detail in the daily work of officers and non-commissioned officers, and any work out in the open after dark, and should, therefore, be practised as much as possible.

Signalling.—The amount of work and time devoted to visual signalling have not borne fruit in this war, but the more practice men have with the telephones and the buzzer the better. An enormous amount is dependent on the telephones. Heavy batteries go in for flag signalling with the Observation Officers.

On the whole peace training is proved to have been on the right lines, but from what has been seen much more might be done with the advanced artillery officer. The Germans are said to use him to a great extent. Much has also to be learnt by artillery in their work in conjunction with aircraft. Some notes on this subject will form a heading in a later communication.

Some notes on conversations with wounded Royal Field Artillery officers at Millbank Hospital.

The German artillery at Mons was very well handled ; as soon as they had located a battery it would be taken on in front, and shortly afterwards would be brought under more or less enfilade fire from batteries to a flank.

The Germans fire high-explosive shell, as well as shrapnel, from their field guns. Their shell is very indifferent and did very little damage, but their fire was very accurate. The shrapnel shells used by the British are superior to those used by the Germans. The high-explosive shells were sometimes used with a time fuze ; the noise was terrific, but effect very local, probably not more than 20 yards each side. Germans fired entirely in bursts of fire ; slow rate of fire never used. Bursts of fire consisted of from about 6 to 12 shells ; as a rule, shells could be heard coming, and it was possible to take cover before they arrived.

When the German infantry got within about 1,500 yards and the English artillery were beginning to get effective fire, our guns were bombarded with terrific rate of fire. Voice control was then no good, and no signaller could stand up. *The telephone was the only thing that was of any use.*

The German fire was greatly assisted by aeroplanes ; they had a very good system of signals, and they gave the line and got the range in a very short time. After the first few days the English aeroplanes began to arrive on the scene and the German aeroplanes then did much less.

When reconnoitring it is inadvisable to take too many officers away from brigades. An instance occurred of only two officers being left with the three batteries, while the rest of the officers of the brigade had gone off to reconnoitre positions for the guns. During their absence a serious crisis arose, which might have led to a serious disaster.

Always have patrols well ahead and well in touch with the brigade. An instance occurred of a brigade advancing into a village, and meeting an ammunition column in a narrow street, which was endeavouring to get back. That is, the two forces met in a narrow street, going in opposite directions. The confusion which ensued would have been avoided had there been a patrol in front of the brigade.

Owing to the distance batteries came into action behind the crest, it was found advisable for the battery commander to plant his own aiming posts.

The Germans, as a rule, search about 400 yards back from the crest—it is therefore advisable to be at least this distance back. It has also usually the advantage of getting less dead ground. The semi-covered position has turned out to be a bad one.

The battery commander should never use an observation limber, or have a limber for cover ; a limber was once put up on the opposite flank to where observation party was, and drew fire from all round, so much so that the limber was never got away. A limber for the ranging officer at the battery is essential.

Section commanders must be as close as they can get behind the shield of the gun nearest the battery commander.

Gun pits or epaulments in the open are quite useless, they merely serve to draw fire—behind cover they are very valuable. Wagons must be placed very close to the guns—placed touching the guns. No space must be left as bullets get through. A good many casualties were thus caused to ammunition numbers. Earth should be piled up about 18 inches high, and a couple of feet in front of the shield to prevent bullets ricocheting through underneath.

Horses were practically never unharnessed. The firing battery wagons should be unhooked, and not, as a rule, unlimbered. The limber gives extra protection, and it is advisable to have as much ammunition as possible at the guns in case of emergency.

Loading numbers *must* keep the shell well covered up until it is in the bore of the gun. An instance occurred of a fuze, before being loaded, being struck by a shrapnel bullet, the result being that the loading number had both arms blown off and the rest of the detachment were knocked out.

If possible, wagon line should be concealed altogether from view under woods, avenues of trees, &c. If this cannot be done, it is advisable to keep the wagon line on the move as long as the ranging aeroplanes are in sight, otherwise heavy fire will be turned on them, and great losses of horses will result.

A method of arranging the ammunition supply which was found useful was to have two first-line wagons close to the flank of the battery, and to use them to keep the firing battery wagons full. This can be done by utilizing the pauses between the bursts of fire—men running up with ammunition in carriers. As soon as these two wagons are empty, they should be removed, the teams hooked in, and be sent back to the ammunition column to refill. It was found best to refill these wagons, and not exchange them with those of the column.

Arrangements should be made in the event of its being desired to open fire again after dark. A lamp should be put well out to a flank to be used after dark as an aiming point, and, in addition, a lantern (in the nature of a bull's-eye lantern) should be placed well to the front of each gun to give it its line of fire, or, if necessary, it can be placed in rear of the gun, if it is well hidden from the enemy. It was by this means that the Germans constantly shelled the bivouacs after dark.

Type of Gun Epaulment for Shielded Gun found suitable at the front.

SECTION OF TRENCH.

Details.

Inside edge of parapet to be revetted with posts and boughs from any suitable trees. The gun and trail platform to be kept as clear as possible.

The trench for spade is backed with any timber available in order that the thrust of the spade may have a good bearing, and not tear up the ground and allow the carriage to run back.

The bottom of the trenches should be covered with straw or boughs, &c., in order to be comfortable for the men at night, and waterproof sheets stretched across the top to protect the men in rainy weather; drainage will be necessary.

The wagon is unlimbered and placed as shown in diagram in order to afford protection from splinters, from back blast of H.E. shell, especially when burst on percussion. Ammunition can be served from trenches or wagons, and an extra wagon body can be left up if necessary to help close the space in rear, and the ammunition from its limber stored in the trench while the limber returns for more from the column.

The whole work must be cunningly concealed by trees and branches in order to defy location by airmen, young trees being stuck in the ground in as natural a manner as possible.

Sacks of earth on top of wagons, parapet, &c., increase the protection considerably.

For the above pattern of protection the cutting tools of a sub-section are sufficient provided that they are in proper order, viz., hand saws properly set, and axes and billhooks sharp. A light crowbar is useful, if procurable.

German tactics.

The following information was obtained from an officer who has been at the front :—

1. The German method of advance is to show a front with cavalry, in close contact with which is a highly mobile force of Jaegers conveyed in motor lorries and accompanied by machine guns. When attacked, the cavalry calls up the

Jaegers who deploy behind the cavalry screen. The cavalry then withdraws, and the allied cavalry finds itself confronted by an infantry force with quick-firers.

2. *German rearguards.*—These consist of perhaps two cavalry regiments, several batteries of artillery, motor mounted machine guns and 1,000 infantry on motor lorries. Each lorry carries about 80 men.

The infantry are rapidly transported from one place to another by means of these lorries. This occurred in rearguard actions and during the fighting on the River Aisne.

3. *German batteries* are distributed when in action, the guns being posted in sections according to the lie of the ground. The various sections are connected by telephone. The range-finder is some distance to the front. Each battery has a powerful telescope and the officers have 6-inch maps.

4. *Machine guns* in a position are combined with wire entanglements as shown in Plate VI. (page 28).

Plate VI.

The apparent gap in the entanglement is purposely made to draw the attacker into the field of fire of the machine gun.

In the encounters which took place in Belgium the Germans on several occasions brought up their machine guns immediately behind their most advanced line of infantry. They hid them (*e.g.*, on the first floor of houses) and allowed the enemy to advance past them and then opened fire on them from the rear. Also in defence machine guns are placed in first floor of houses. The French were ordered to shell all villages before attacking.

4. *Aeroplanes* direct the German artillery fire, particularly the fire of howitzers—our guns must be concealed by branches of trees, &c.

5. *Entrenchments.*—The Germans since the beginning of the war have made the greatest use of field entrenchments. The extent and the strength of the positions which they have prepared entail an attack upon them which approximates to regular siege operations.

The methods adopted in the German positions taken up on our front are in no sense hastily improvised but show a carefully thought out system.

The method adopted is as follows :—

(*a.*) To render the positions as inconspicuous as possible to patrols and aircraft.

(*b.*) To alter the natural surface of the ground as little as possible, and where these trenches cannot be concealed to prepare dummy trenches along the whole front in order to give a uniform appearance.

(*c.*) To hide the trenches and gun emplacements by means of branches, coloured canvas and plants, taking care that such alterations are not conspicuous to an observer.

The difficulties of reconnaissance experienced by aircraft have shown how carefully their system has been carried out.

The design of trench nearly always adopted is a very deep trench with parados and traverses for protection against shell fire and trenches in rear for supports joined to trenches in front by deep zig-zag trenches.

Their trenches have been designed in anticipation of a prolonged occupation with observation posts, certain portions sheltered from overhead fire, drainage arrangements, excavated niches for rations, kit, ammunition, maps, search lights, star shells, &c.

Dummy trenches, or trenches manned by dummies, are also used in front of the true position. The trenches actually occupied are concealed, and between them and the dummy trenches are wire entanglements, swept by fire from the former.

The attached plates are examples of some of the German designs for trenches. Plates VII. to XI.

6. *Wire entanglements.*—Different types employed :—

(*a.*) Very low pickets, 4 inches to 2 feet 3 inches high.
(*b.*) Normal, pickets, 5 feet high.

These are placed about 50 yards from the trench, carefully disguised and hidden by a glacis in front.

NOTE.—All these works are carefully covered up and disguised with branches, straw, and grass and made to look exactly like the surrounding country.

7. *German artillery.*—Some notes on German artillery are attached in Appendix B.

STAFF WORK.

1. *Orders.*—Complaints are frequent about the delay in obtaining receipt for orders. The best course to be adopted, if in scattered billets, is to deliver orders by an officer in motor car.

Staff officers should invariably get the receipt obtained for an order brought to them by whoever delivers the order.

It is never safe to trust to any form of verbal order or verbal arrangements : the most reliable messengers have been found to fail to deliver them or misinterpreted what was intended.

Starting point.—It has been found that troops require a great deal of marshalling to get everyone into their places at the starting point. No amount of writing seems to do this with units large or small coming in from various directions.

Energetic staff work on the spot is the only way. The starting point should be reconnoitred on the ground before it is given out in orders to see there is room on the road which will allow vehicles being pulled out of the way on to the side in order to leave room for the troops to pass.

It is difficult for a brigade staff to send an officer very often to headquarters for orders ; often nothing but a tired horse or a borrowed signaller's bicycle is available.

Some brigade headquarters have found it essential to have a guard, with sentry, to ensure being wakened at the proper time during the night or early morning before movement.

2. *Billeting.*—When troops are billeted in depth and brigade and divisional headquarters are situated in rear it is advisable, in order to allow the headquarters to get to the head of the column to fix a definite time for the headquarters to pass the starting point and arrange for the fighting troops to fit in behind.

When approaching billeting areas the transport (1st line also) generally halts in the middle of the village and blocks the roads. This must be prevented.

It is most important that billeting officers should select, without delay, brigade, battalion, and company places respectively, where the transport is to halt while the detail of billets are being worked out.

Brigade billeting officers must rapidly select battalion and company billeting areas before the troops arrive and allow the latter to proceed at once into their billets and clear the roads.

3. *Demolitions.*—There have been complaints from Royal Engineer field companies that sufficient warning is not given to prepare bridges for demolition. Preparations of this sort take time. There have been failures in this owing to divisional orders arriving too late.

4. *Supplies.*—The issue of supplies, especially fresh meat and groceries, does not seem to have worked very well. It was understood that supplies would arrive in mechanical transport at brigade refilling points, packed in bulk for the brigade, and that it would there be divided up amongst brigade headquarters and the four battalions. It has been found that there is a scarcity both in men and implements at brigade refilling points to enable this to be done. This, therefore, needs very careful arrangement.

It has been found that Army Form B 55 (Ration Indent) was only being handed in on the same day, in fact, at same time as supplies are drawn. This is running things too fine, and arrangements are needed to remedy this.

The supply, personnel and materiel has been very over-taxed in issuing daily supplies, with the result that wagons have been kept waiting many hours at refilling points, and then often have returned empty. Careful organization is needed to prevent a breakdown.

5. *Ordnance, pay, &c.*—There was at first a general lack of knowledge as to the machinery for obtaining cash for pay, the execution of ordnance services, remounts, repairs, requisitions on local resources, or how payment is to be recovered for work done by local tradesmen, &c. Lack of previous clear-cut arrangements all adds to the amount of written work which has to be done.

In the 1st Division the arrangement made for repairs to wagons, &c., was as follows :—

Each brigade major was given 5*l.* imprest account. Repairs when done by local workmen were reported to the Assistant Director of Ordnance Services, who paid direct in cash. If the brigades, however, were out of touch with divisional headquarters, such services by local tradesmen were paid in cash and a receipt sent to the Assistant Director of Ordnance Services, who reimbursed the brigade major or other individual who paid the bill.

Units are ordered to indent on Assistant Director of Ordnance Services for any requirements ; if not immediately met, these indents enable the Assistant Director of Ordnance Services to look ahead and do the best he can to meet urgent demands.

6. *Discipline.*—March discipline easily becomes slack, straggling has to be rigidly guarded against. Men fall out on the march into cafes, &c. March discipline must be kept at all hazards, otherwise battalions and companies get very short of fighting men.

7. *Sick horses.*—Considerable trouble has been caused by units leaving lame horses, &c., scattered about the country. The Assistant Director of Veterinary Services should co-ordinate the work and collect the horses in one spot as far as possible.

8. *Intelligence.*—Very interesting information relating to lines of march, order of battle, &c., may be found in the

pocket books and personal diaries of German prisoners, or even on the bodies of their dead.

Our soldiers should be cautioned against carrying among their private papers any information which might, in the event of their falling into the enemy's hand, afford intelligence to the latter regarding the movements and composition of the allied armies.

9. *Uniforms.*—The following applies to men of all arms and to every branch of the German Army :—

The number of the army corps, regiment, battalion and company is marked, together with the man's personal number inside the lining of the tunic.

B.A. XV = Bekleidungsamt (clothing department) of the XVth Army Corps.

Identity discs show whether a man belongs to the Standing Army, the Reserve or the Landwehr.

R.I.R. = Infantry Regiment No. 98, Arms (rifles and bayonets) are marked in the same manner.

10. *Instructions for military police.*—An example of instructions, as issued by the 5th Division for military police, is attached in Appendix A as a guide.

11. *Dress.*—It has been found that men have been in the habit of wearing unauthorized articles with their uniform, and of giving away cap badges, shoulder straps, &c., and also articles of equipment not required at the moment. Orders against this require to be very strictly enforced.

12. *Courts-martial.*—Many irregularities have occurred through the difficulty of obtaining a copy of the Manual of Military Law. It is therefore recommended that all officers should record in their note books a few details as to procedure, particularly as regards field general courts-martial, *e.g.*, that it is necessary to record in writing sufficient evidence to prove the charges.

13. *Returns.*—It is important that Army Form B 213 should be rendered punctually by units to Deputy-Adjutant-General, 3rd Echelon, Base, as it is by means of this return that next-of-kin are informed of casualties. This return can only be made up accurately by units after a roll-call. It is, therefore, necessary that a duplicate of a nominal roll should be kept by each company on the person, and another

copy with the baggage section of the train. The roll should be called at the earliest opportunity and casualties reported at once.

14. *First field dressings.*—It is found that men are in the habit of using their first field dressing to tie up minor cuts, &c. Also when dressing a wounded man they use their own field dressing instead of that on the wounded man, and thus become deficient of their own dressing. Special instructions appear to be necessary to stop this practice.

15. *Iron rations.*—Care is necessary to see that men retain their iron rations intact. An impression exists that the iron ration consists of two squares of Oxo and a tin of groceries, and it should be made clear that the tin of preserved meat, &c., is also part of the ration.

16. *Officers' kits.*—As the baggage section of the train may be out of touch with units for days at a time, officers are recommended to be independent of it as regards some warm clothing for the night, washing and shaving articles, &c.

17. *Water.*—A good deal of water is to be found in most villages, and it is as a rule fit to drink. The practice of filling water bottles direct from the pumps is wasteful and should not be allowed. Mess tins or buckets should be filled from the pump and the water bottle filled from them.

18. *Refilling.*—It is often impossible to carry out refilling of trains from tail board to tail board. It is generally found more convenient for supply columns to deposit their stores on the ground and for supply sections of the train to refill from the heaps thus made. By this method the supply column is able to return to railhead immediately.

19. *Local supplies.*—A scale of local charges drawn up by the French authorities is available for inspection at the Mairie of each village. Draught oxen have been found very good to eat, as owing to the war they have not been worked for some time and are in soft condition. At least one pair should be left to work on each farm, and as the pairs are accustomed to work together, odd numbers should not be taken.

General information.

1. The 3rd Infantry Brigade says "Axol" lamp has proved invaluable.

2. It is recommended that all troops, both officers and men, should carry tea and some sort of "billy" to boil water in and drink out of. The food wagons often do not come up and all that can be got is the tea made in a "billy" and the biscuits that each carries in his haversack.

3. It is dangerous to touch the heads of the German un-exploded 10·5 cm. (4·13-inch) shell.

Note.—This probably refers to the universal shell used in light field howitzer ; *see* Appendix B (*b*).

Notes from the diary of a private individual travelling in Belgium during the latter part of August and the month of September.

The German army as a piece of machinery has been almost perfected. The only mistake that has been made is that of disregarding the human element, and the taking for granted that the one great essential for the success of the military operations—Time—will work out according to the pre-arranged schedule. One very interesting and novel feature is apparent. Infantry, regarded as infantry alone, solely dependent upon mobility, and accurate rifle fire, initiative, and what the French term *élan*, has been subordinated to mass movements. An infantry regiment is employed merely as a support for artillery and for the machine gun. In the 1st and 2nd line troops I should judge that 10 to 12 Maxim guns are attached to every infantry regiment. They are handled and transported as regimental transport. A regiment of German infantry could pass through a town, and an observer reporting on their passage would swear that he had seen no machine guns of any kind.

Ambulances.—The ambulance service also is most interesting. On entering the towns all motor cabs or other suitable vehicles are taken ; such vehicles, including the ordinary taxicab, are very rapidly transformed into an ambulance capable of carrying at least eight wounded men. This is done by a force of carpenters and machinists who simply remove the body from the chassis and substitute a frame of wood covered with canvas. The wounded are generally brought into hospitals at night—for it is the policy of the Germans to conceal their losses in every way, both from their own men and from the inhabitants. (Sketch, Plate III., attached.)

Machine guns.—The gun as it rests on the ground (Plate I., Figure A) is about the height of a man in the firing position lying down. When raised (Plate I., Figure B) it is about the height of a man kneeling. A spectator saw 50 of these guns loaded into small two-wheeled carts and into motor trucks, which are mentioned later ; the operation of loading took less than 35 minutes. As they passed through a town no one would have detected from any evidence that any machine guns had been taken through the streets. The machine gun is sometimes carried in the manner of an African hammock on the shoulders of bearers. They move it also carrying it as they would a stretcher (Plate I., Figure C), with a blanket thrown over the gun and a couple of knapsacks or perhaps an ammunition box ; when carried in this manner the gunners at a distance are easily mistaken for stretcher-bearers carrying a wounded man off the field.

Plate II., Figure A, contains hasty sketches of the two-wheeled cart which is fitted to transport three of these guns. They have two men to every gun, The driver and another man ride on the seat, and each cart is accompanied by a mounted non-commissioned officer or, perhaps, subaltern.

The members of this mobile machine-gun force march light, their knapsacks, blankets, and in some cases their rifles, being carried in the carts. The mounted men that accompany them have a rope and leather harness, so that the horse can be used as the leader of a tandem in case of heavy going. The cart has strong and steady springs. The appearance of the cart with its load of, in some cases, bundles of forage, knapsacks, haversacks and blankets, would attract not the slightest attention. The guns at the bottom were absolutely hidden. The cart is somewhat like an English butcher's cart, only much heavier. The tail-board drops down in the ordinary way.

In regard to the motor vans, they carry nine guns, placed as shown in the sketch. (Plate II., Figure B.) The vans have evidently a shallow false bottom. This is very carefully concealed, so carefully indeed, that it is said that some of these lorries have been captured and lost without the guns having been discovered by the captors. A small tail-board, which drops down, facilitates the guns being hauled out or replaced. A heavy load is placed on top of the false bottom. The sides of these motor vans are quite high, and in many cases I saw machine-gun detachments of no less than 15 or 16 men carried on a van.

The use and mobility of machine guns carried in this manner is, of course, apparent. They are always up with the regiment, and can be taken over any ground without difficulty to support an advance or cover a retreat. Moreover, if necessary, they can be concealed from falling into the hands of an enemy by digging a shallow grave, wrapping the gun, &c., in a blanket, and covering the whole with a few shovelfulls of earth.* The two spikes (Plate I., Figure D) are used to fasten down the foot-plates of the machine-gun mounting. They can be driven into the floor of buildings and into the interstices of cobble-stones, besides being used in ordinary ground. Each pair is connected with a strap or a chain.

The ammunition boxes are carried under the seat of the wagon and are probably concealed somewhere in the motor van.

The ammunition is probably carried in what appears to be the trailer to an ordinary two-wheeled cart.

Entrenchments.—Plate **IV.** gives a plan of some German trenches and the way they have arranged their wire entanglements. These are drawn from some examined near Liege, where the Germans have had time to entrench very carefully.

---

* Machine guns have actually been found buried in this manner. It is understood that the wooden cross marking their sites had a slight distinguishing mark.

APPENDIX A.

PRELIMINARY INSTRUCTIONS FOR THE MILITARY POLICE, 5TH DIVISION.

1. *General.*—The usual routine police duties will be continued at the peace station pending entrainment. The military police will make themselves acquainted with the names or numbers of the various units comprising the division, and with the names and ranks (and, as far as possible, the personal appearance) of officers of the headquarters of the division, and of headquarters of artillery and infantry brigades.

2. *Command.*—In the absence of the Assistant Provost-Marshal, military police attached to the headquarters of artillery and infantry brigades will act under the direction of the staff captains of those brigades.

3. *Duties on march.*—On the march, the non-commissioned officer and military police attached to the headquarters of the two rearmost infantry brigades will invariably march with, and in rear of, the baggage section of the divisional train, and will prevent straggling. Stragglers and animals will be collected and march back to their units at the first opportunity. Stray animals not identified will be handed over to the nearest mounted unit. No man except the driver is to be allowed to ride on a wagon, unless provided with a pass signed by the transport officer. When passing through towns and villages the military police will march in rear of the formations to which they are attached, collect and bring on all stragglers.

4. *Sale of liquor.*—Non-commissioned officers and men of the division are forbidden to enter any hotel, inn, or restaurant abroad for the purpose of buying liquor of any kind. The proprietors of such places (which are placed out of bounds) will be warned not to sell liquor to the troops, and the names and addresses of any proprietors or purchasers infringing this rule will be noted and reported to the Assistant Provost-Marshal.

5. Close touch and mutual co-operation will be maintained between the military police attached to the headquarters of formations and the regimental police belonging to the units of those formations.

6. Great care will be taken to protect the persons and property of the inhabitants from any violence or plundering, and they are to be treated courteously.

7. The military police will always endeavour to get into touch with and co-operate with the civil police in maintaining order.

8. *Illegal requisitioning.*—Only supply officers, Army Service Corps, and ordnance officers are authorised to make requisitions for supplies and material, &c., for current requirements.

Indiscriminate requisitioning by other individual officers, warrant officers, non-commissioned officers and men and the granting of requisition receipt notes, is strictly forbidden and will be treated as plundering under the Army Act.

9. *Sutlers.*—Traders and sutlers endeavouring to accompany and deal with the troops, unless provided with a pass signed by the Assistant Provost Marshal, will be placed in custody and handed over to the civil police.

10. *Powers of arrest.*—The military police may at any time arrest and detain for trial persons, subject to the military law, committing offences, and are authorised in cases of emergency to call on any troops to assist them by supplying them with guards, sentries, or patrols.

11. *Charge reports.*—When handing over an offender to his unit for disposal, care will be taken to hand in a charge report at the same time. A duplicate charge report will be rendered to the non-commissioned officer i/c of the detachment of military police and by him to the Assistant Provost Marshal. It is particularly necessary that the names and addresses of all civilians whom the military police may have to give in custody, or call as witnesses, should be carefully noted at the time, and also the names of the places where they may be found. The military police will likewise take steps to procure at the time (or within 24 hours) a charge report duly signed for each person handed over to them for custody.

12. *Field punishment.*—When an offender is handed over to the military police for execution of sentence of field punishment, or otherwise, a return is to be rendered by the officer by whom he is handed over showing the name and description of the offender, the offence, the date of award of punishment, the punishment awarded, and the name of the awarding officer. A committal warrant is not required for a sentence of field punishment. A register will be kept by the non-commissioned officer in charge of the military police with each formation of all punishments inflicted by them and how the offenders were disposed of after punishment. An extract dealing with the period from Sunday to Saturday will be sent to the Assistant Provost Marshal each Sunday morning.

13. *Billeting parties.*—Two military police from divisional headquarters and one from the headquarters of each infantry brigade will accompany the billeting parties daily, and will march in rear of the advanced guard. On arrival in their respective billeting areas they will see that the water supply is not fouled, and will ascertain the situations of hotels, liquor shops, houses of ill repute, and houses containing cases of infectious disease, and report them to the Assistant Provost Marshal or staff captains with a view to their being placed out of bounds, and guards placed over them if necessary. They will make themselves acquainted with the position of headquarters offices of the division or brigade and of hospitals, &c.

14. *Billets. bivouacs.*—The military police will patrol billeting or bivouac areas from the time of arrival until half an hour after "lights out" in order to maintain order and prevent men leaving their billeting areas without permission, or other irregularities. When billets or bivouacs are vacated the military police will remain behind and see that no loose papers or other things are left behind which would give any clue to the designation or numbers of the formations that have occupied the billets over night.

APPENDIX B.

GERMAN ARTILLERY.

Horse and field artillery have the same 15-pr. field gun (1896). Field howitzer batteries are armed with a new light howitzer (1909).

(a.) The *field gun* is the old .15-pr. converted and mounted on a shielded gun-recoil carriage.

Calibre, 3·03 inches.

Range with time fuze up to 5,500 yards.

Range with percussion fuze up to 9,186 yards.

Maximum rate of fire, 20 rounds a minute.

Ammunition.—Shrapnel or H.E.

H.E. is being replaced by a universal shell.

Weight of shrapnel or H.E. is 15 pounds.

Contains 300 bullets (45 to the pound).

H.E. shell contains 7 oz. of nitro powder with fulminate detonator.

Rounds per gun in battery, 132. In ammunition columns per gun, 246.

(b.) The *light field howitzer*, issued in 1910.

Calibre, 4·13 inches.

Rate of fire, at least 6 rounds a minute.

Time fuze range up to 5,800 yards.

Percussion, 8,100 yards.

Ammunition.—Shrapnel and H.E. which are to be replaced by universal shell as soon as the present stock is exhausted.

Weight of shrapnel or H.E., 31 lbs.

Weight of universal shell, 31 lbs. (nearly).

A universal shell for howitzers contains 500 bullets (42 to the pound), 5¼ ozs. of picric acid with fulminate detonator.

When burst on percussion the high-explosive bursters in the head and among the bullets detonate, giving the effect of a powerful mine shell.

Rounds per gun in battery, 91.

Rounds per gun in ammunition column, 147.

(c.) *Heavy field howitzer battery* (4 howitzers in a battery).—15 *cm.* (5·9 *inch*) *heavy field howitzer* is mounted on an old type of heavy limbered carriage.   Pattern 1902.   Weight behind the team about 2¼ tons.

Maximum range, 8,150 yards.   Effective range, 6,000 yards

Rate of fire, 2 or 3 rounds per minute.

Ammunition —H.E. shell weighs 89 lb.

Percussion fuzes, with or without delaying action. are employed. Bursting charge is 11 lb.

Rounds per howitzer in the battery, 72.

Rounds per howitzer in ammunition column, 360.

(d.) 21 *cm.* (8·27-*inch*) *mortar battery.*—This mortar is really a breech-loading howitzer.

Maximum range, 8,400 yards.

Ammunition.—Weight of H.E. shell, 262 lb.

Rounds per gun in battery, nil.

Rounds per gun in ammunition column, 173.

(e.) *Siege Artillery.*—

(i.) 28 *cm.* (11-*inch howitzer*).   *Range* 12,000 *yards.*

It was reported in March, 1913, that there were 6 batteries each of 2 of these howitzers, but according .to a Belgian officer who was at Namur in August, 1914, there were 30 batteries of these guns.

Reports have also been received in 1913, of a 32 cm. (12½-inch) howitzer being introduced.

(ii.) 42 *cm.* (16½-*inch*) *howitzer,*

It is reported that there are 10 of these in the German Army and that they are manned by Krupp's men.   Their length is about 12 feet and the height of the shell is 5 feet 1 inch.   Wagons with cement to make platforms accompany the men.

Two of these are reported now about Lille.

Plate I.

SKETCH OF MACHINE GUN AND MOUNT.

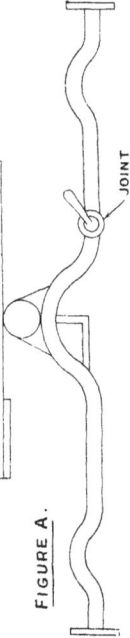

FIGURE A.

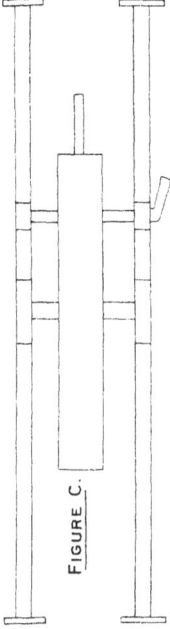

FIGURE B.

JOINT

FIGURE C.

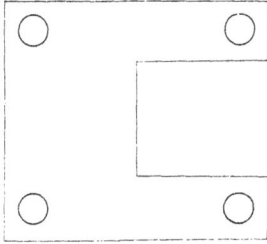

FIGURE D.

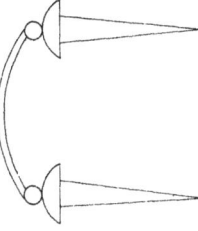

FIGURE D.

SPIKES
ATTACHED TO STRAP
OR CHAIN.

Malby&Sons Lith

36840.J/0600. 1/45.

Plate. II.

MACHINE GUNS IN MOTOR TRUCK.

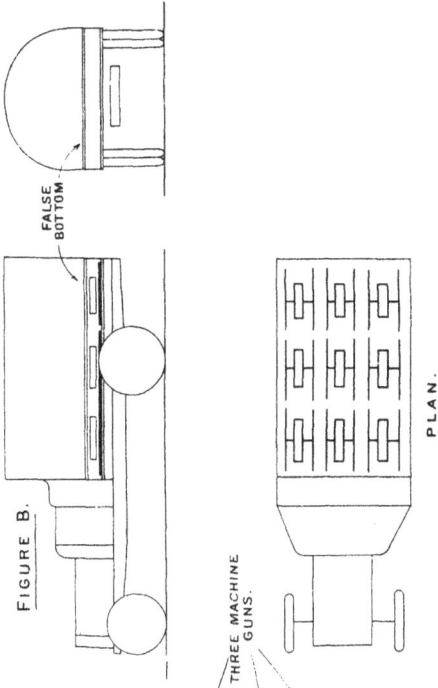

GALLOPING CART CONTAINING THREE GUNS.

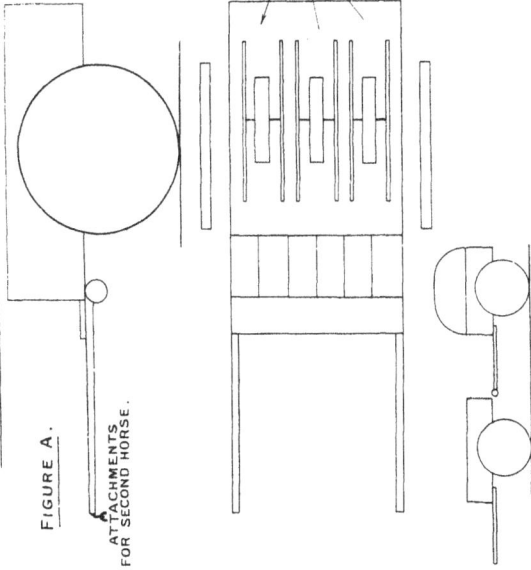

FIGURE A.

FIGURE B.

FALSE BOTTOM

THREE MACHINE GUNS.

ATTACHMENTS FOR SECOND HORSE.

PLAN.

Malby & Sons Lith.

Plate III.

TAXI CAB AMBULANCE TO CARRY 8 WOUNDED.

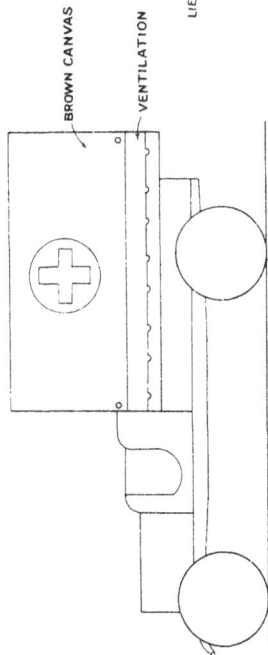

SECTION OF BODY SHEWING DOUBLE DECK

STRETCHERS

PLAN.

WOUNDED TO LIE ATHWARTSHIPS

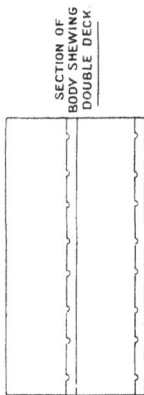

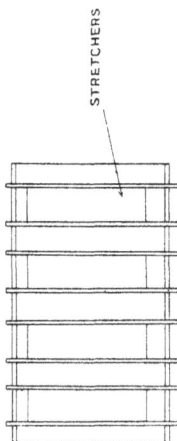

BROWN CANVAS

VENTILATION

Malby&Sons Lith

3530

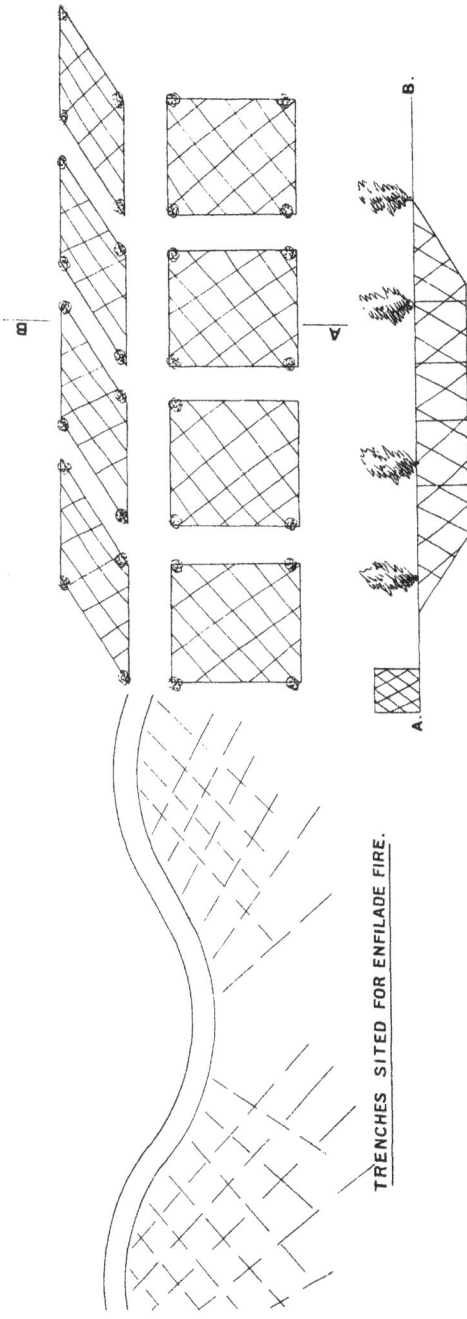

TRENCHES SITED FOR ENFILADE FIRE.

SECTION OF ENTANGLEMENTS THROUGH LINE A.B.
(SCALE—SLIGHTLY DIFFERENT.)

A.

B.

Malby & Sons, Lith.

Plate VII.

PLAN OF GERMAN TRENCHES DESIGNED FOR
A BATTALION WITH EMPLACEMENTS FOR
MACHINE-GUN FLANKING FIRE.

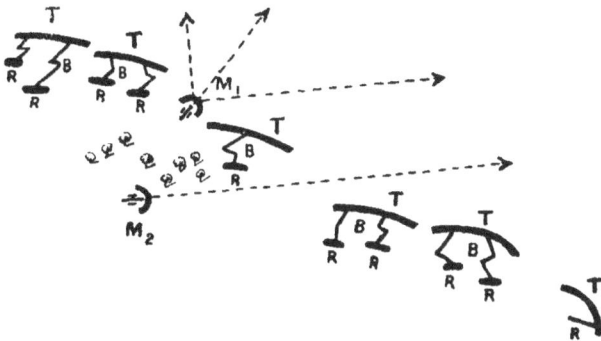

T. Rifle trenches.
R. Trenches for supports.
M. Machine-gun emplacements.
B. Communication trenches.

44

Plate VIII.

DESIGN OF DEEP RIFLE TRENCHES.

(a) Profile

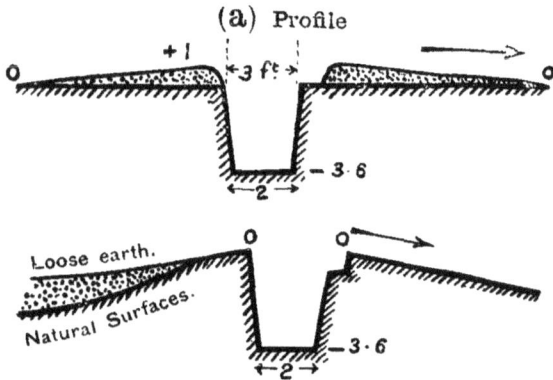

NOTE.—The loose earth which is thrown behind the Trench is covered with grass or straw.

(b) Traversed Trenches.

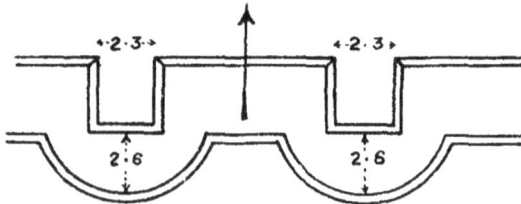

The slopes of the traverses are revetted with planks.

Plate IX.

SUPPORT AND COMMUNICATION TRENCHES.

(a.) Trenches for Supports.

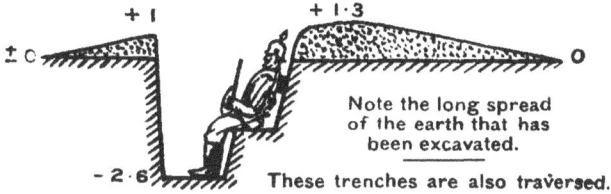

+ 1   + 1·3

± 0   0

Note the long spread
of the earth that has
been excavated.

- 2·6

These trenches are also traversed.

(b.) Communication Trenches.

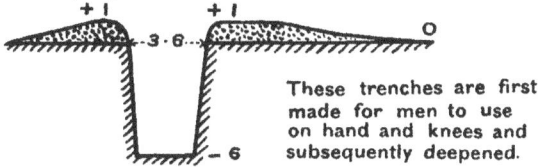

+ 1   + 1

- 3·6

O

These trenches are first
made for men to use
on hand and knees and
subsequently deepened.

- 6

(c.) Combined Trenches.

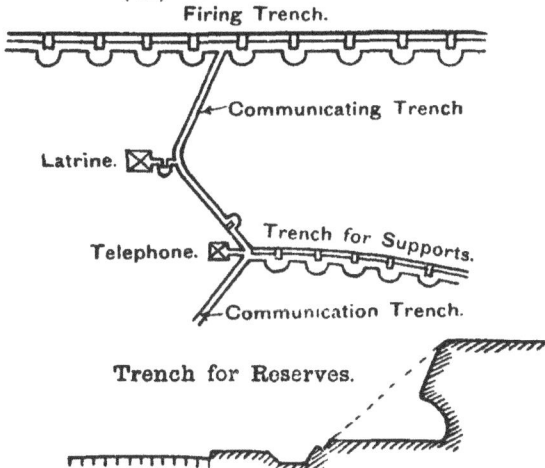

Firing Trench.

←Communicating Trench

Latrine. ⊠

Telephone. ⊠

Trench for Supports.

←Communication Trench.

Trench for Reserves.

Plate X.

MACHINE-GUN EMPLACEMENT.

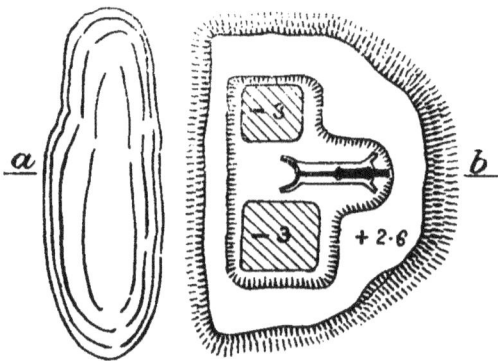

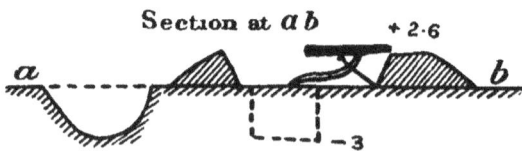

Section at ab +2·6

Plate **XI**.

EPAULMENT FOR FIELD ARTILLERY **AS THROWN**
UP DURING AN ENGAGEMENT.

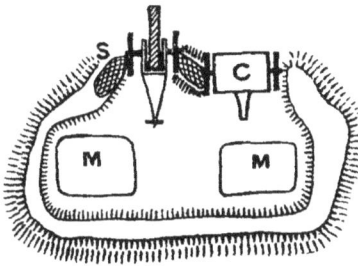

M. Trench for gunners.
S. Sandbags.
C. Limber.

This design is improved by lateral covered shelters.

(B11111) Wt. w 10628—1488 10 M 1/15 H & S 1383wo

www.ingramcontent.com/pod-product-compliance
Lightning Source LLC
Chambersburg PA
CBHW020952030426
42339CB00004B/63